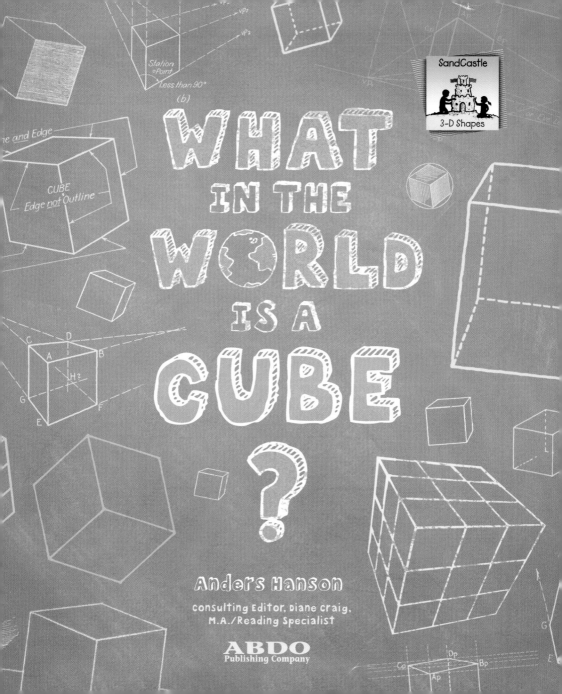

SandCastle
3-D Shapes

WHAT IN THE WORLD IS A CUBE?

Anders Hanson

Consulting Editor, Diane Craig,
M.A./Reading Specialist

ABDO
Publishing Company

Published by ABDO Publishing Company, 8000 West 78th Street, Edina, MN 55439.

Copyright © 2008 by Abdo Consulting Group, Inc. International copyrights reserved in all countries.

No part of this book may be reproduced in any form without written permission from the publisher. SandCastle™ is a trademark and logo of ABDO Publishing Company.

Printed in the United States.
Editor: Pam Price
Curriculum Coordinator: Nancy Tuminelly
Cover and Interior Design and Production: Mighty Media
Photo Credits: Image 100, JupiterImages Corporation, ShutterStock

Library of Congress Cataloging-in-Publication Data

Hanson, Anders, 1980-
  What in the world is a cube? / Anders Hanson.
    p. cm. -- (3-D shapes)
  ISBN 978-1-59928-887-1
  1. Cube--Juvenile literature. 2. Shapes--Juvenile literature. 3. Geometry, Solid--Juvenile literature.
I. Title.

QA491.H358 2008
516'.156--dc22
                        2007010192

SandCastle™ Level: Transitional

Emerging Readers	Beginning Readers	Transitional Readers	Fluent Readers
(no flags)	(1 flag)	(2 flags)	(3 flags)

SandCastle™ would like to hear from you. Please send us your comments or questions.

sandcastle@abdopublishing.com

SandCastle™ books are created by a team of professional educators, reading specialists, and content developers around five essential components—phonemic awareness, phonics, vocabulary, text comprehension, and fluency—to assist young readers as they develop reading skills and strategies and increase their general knowledge. All books are written, reviewed, and leveled for guided reading, early reading intervention, and Accelerated Reader® programs for use in shared, guided, and independent reading and writing activities to support a balanced approach to literacy instruction. The Sand-Castle™ series has four levels that correspond to early literacy development. The levels are provided to help teachers and parents select appropriate books for young readers.

www.abdopublishing.com

3-D shapes are all around us.

3-D stands for 3-dimensional.
It means that an object is not flat.

A cube is a 3-D shape.

WIDTH

DEPTH

HEIGHT

HEIGHT = WIDTH = DEPTH

It has three equal dimensions, height, width, and depth.

A cube has six identical
square faces.

Only three of them can
be visible at a time.

Cubes are everywhere!

Katy has a present
for her mother.

The present is
cube shaped.

Diced tofu is cube shaped.

Have you ever eaten tofu?

Maria and her parents
play a board game
with dice.

Dice are cube shaped.

This clock is shaped like a cube.

Can you tell time?

13

Pool chalk is cube shaped.

Have you ever played pool?

Josh plays with
big, yellow blocks.

The blocks are
shaped like cubes.

This 3-D puzzle is in the shape of a cube.

Have you ever done a 3-D puzzle?

Find the cube!

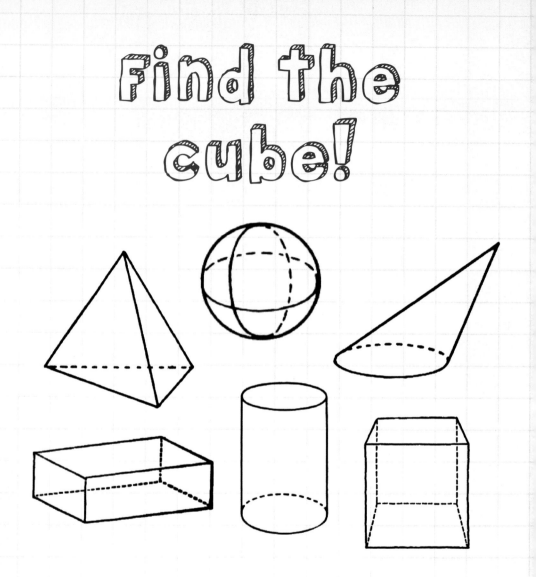

Which one of these 3-D shapes is a cube?

How many cubes can you find in this photo?

Everyday cubes

Take a look around you.
Do you see any cubes?

How to draw a cube

1. Draw a square.

2. Draw a right angle next to the square.

3. Connect the right angle and the square with three straight lines.

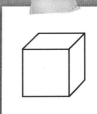

Glossary

dimensional – having a measurement of length, width, or thickness.

face – one of the polygons, such as a square, rectangle, or triangle, that make a 3-D shape. The faces of a cube are squares.

identical – exactly the same.

pool – a game played on a table by hitting a ball with the tip of a stick.

right angle – an angle that measures 90 degrees.

tofu – a soft food made from soybeans.

To see a complete list of SandCastle™ books and other nonfiction titles from ABDO Publishing Company, visit www.abdopublishing.com.
8000 West 78th Street, Edina, MN 55439 · 800-800-1312 · 952-831-1632 fax